Wedding Vow Writing

HOW TO WRITE THE MOST ORIGINAL
TEAR-INDUCING, NON-BORING WEDDING VOWS
OF ALL TIME

For Z.

Table of Contents

Preface

It all started when I was thirteen. If you didn't already know, middle school girls are dealt a rough hand. Awkwardly becoming aware of changing body parts, experiencing every feeling on the spectrum without an emotional vocabulary, and falling in love with complete strangers are just a fraction of what we go through. I'll never forget the trauma of learning Josh Hartnett was eleven years older than me...and had a girlfriend. Forever out of reach.

To cope with the melodrama of my new, adolescent season of life, I stopped watching *Pearl Harbor* and turned to creative writing. Sure, I had been journaling in my *Rugrats* diary since the third grade, but this was a new venture. Songs, poems, and even short stories became sources of comfort and therapy.

Little did I know, I was training myself to eventually write about the complex, emotional, and hard-to-describe experiences of life.

Although I'm glad none of my early work was ever published, I am thankful to have started young. My English teacher, Mr. Mitchell, told me during my junior year of high school that I had a gift for writing, and I went on to major in Communication at Baylor University. But my favorite writing challenge of all came at the age of twenty-one after I became engaged.

That's when my fiancé and I decided to write our own wedding vows.

I bought a Tiffany-Blue Moleskine notebook and wrote almost every day during our six-month engagement, enthralled by the opportunity to have a platform to share my words with a large group of family and friends. Every entry had a different feel that reflected the state of our relationship that day; whether we were on cloud nine or drowning in doubts about our relationship didn't matter. I was committed to writing the most authentic wedding vows that I could, and that meant writing about even the less-than-romantic experiences of happily ever after.

The morning of my wedding, I completed my vows covered in bubbles and with pruney fingertips…in a bathtub. Although I don't recommend waiting until the last minute to complete your vows (or bringing notebooks into your bath), I will say that it was the perfect way to start my morning, reflecting on the prior six months and dreaming about the new journey that was about to begin.

I first presented the vows to my six bridesmaids, huddled together on a king-sized mattress in our bridal suite. The praise, tears, and emotional embraces that ensued were a sweet surprise—not only because my hard work had been validated but also because I didn't really have time for revisions.

Then, there I was, holding my notebook with shaky hands and reading the most important words of my life. I could see the smiles of the groomsmen and hear sniffling in the crowd as I focused on the teary eyes of my groom. The moment was transcendent, its significance held at the front of my mind and felt in the depths of my soul. A new journey was beginning, and there was no one in the world I'd rather walk alongside.

My thirteen-year-old self would have been so proud…and she probably would've shed a few less tears for Josh Hartnett if she'd known about the studly groom waiting for her at the end of the aisle only nine years later.

For weeks, I received compliments on the wedding vows I'd worked so hard on. I felt encouraged as both a newlywed and a writer. The amount I learned from the process of writing those vows was unexpected, and while you can't really be a professional wedding vow writer, I consider myself more than qualified to help others who find themselves intimidated by the idea of pouring their hearts out on paper and formulating lifelong promises.

Writing original vows isn't a privilege reserved only for experienced writers. I wrote this book because I believe that every couple has a story worthy of being told on their wedding day, and they should have the tools to be able to tell it. With a little guidance, any couple can write original, tear-inducing, non-boring wedding vows.

Introduction

Ah, wedding vows…the most romantic part of the ceremony.

Sure, the processional and the first kiss are a close second, but there's nothing quite like the exchange of lifelong promises between lovers in front of a crowd. They're as enchanting as they are significant, and when they're done well, even the cynics will be brought to tears.

Up to this point, you've been the misty-eyed wedding guest eagerly awaiting the delivery of the vows, or you've been the guest who can't stop thinking about the cupcake buffet long enough to pay attention to them. Either way, you've only been a guest…until now.

Now, your big day is on the horizon, and you want to write the most original, tear-inducing, non-boring wedding vows of all time—vows that will captivate even the most cupcake-obsessed wedding guest.

You might be asking the following questions: Is it possible for a novice to write vows like that? Or are such vows reserved for professionals?

Yes, and no.

If you're a professional, here's the formula: You start with structure, mix in some vulnerability and a few short stories, pile on the romance, sprinkle in a little humor, and voila. Your guests are drowning in tears before they even know what hit them.

If you're not a professional, you're probably wondering if that formula thing was a joke. And if it was a joke, then why wasn't it funny? And that would be a good question without a good answer.

All questions and writing experience aside, if you're holding this book, you're looking to step up your vow-writing game. And you're in the right place.

This book includes a series of short stories about couples that decided to write their own wedding vows, the obstacles they had to overcome, and the lessons that can be learned from them. You'll learn everything from vow structure to the kinds of comments that shouldn't be said in front of your wedding guests. There's even a section that'll teach you how to make your vows sound like you wrote them instead of like you borrowed lines from Jim and Pam on *The Office*.

Ideally, you're starting this process several months before your wedding date. If you procrastinated, relax, because everything is going to be fine. Unless your wedding is tomorrow or later this afternoon; then, everything is *not* going to be fine, and you should put this book down and Google wedding vows before it's too late. There's no hope for you.

If you're reading this book, you're likely in one of three camps:

1. You're entertaining the idea of writing your own vows, and you're doing your research. You could be swayed in either direction, but you're kind of hoping for a strong gust of wind to make the decision for you.

2. You and your partner have decided together to write your own vows, and the first decision of your marriage was made in harmony (congrats). All you need is a little guidance and/or a kick in the pants.

3. You've been asked by your partner to write your own wedding vows, and you received this book because, despite your kicking and screaming, it's going to happen.

This book is for all of you, although each camp will glean something different. There's plenty of information for the researchers, guidance for the decided couples, and encouragement for the reluctant writers. It's even peppered with humor to ease the pain.

It's a brave choice (even if it was forced on you) to write your own wedding vows. And if they're going to be original, tear-inducing, and non-boring, you'll need to be honest and vulnerable with your fiancé and your wedding guests. Researcher and storyteller Brené Brown says that vulnerability "sounds like truth and feels like courage,"[1] but it also kind of feels like someone punched you in the stomach. There's really no way around that part.

Be sure to purchase the companion journal for this edition, *Wedding Vow Journal: Your guide to the most original, tear-inducing, non-boring wedding vows of all time,* for the most beneficial writing experience. By the end of this process, you'll have the tools and the confidence you need to write the wedding vows that you were born to write.

Now it's time to get to work.

First up

Dwayne & Lane

You couldn't blame Dwayne. He grew up in Texas with an English teacher for a mother. He knew to always place "I" before "E" except after "C," and he could define "gerund" with ease. Dwayne's mother also taught him that "the pen is mightier than the sword,"[2] a worldview surprisingly unappreciated by his deer-hunting, football-worshipping peers, who aptly observed, "It's harder to kill stuff with a pen."

Adolescence was hard on Dwayne, as it usually is for creative types, but thanks to a new generation of Millennials, his uphill battle became a downhill ride after high school. Who knew third-wave-coffee-sipping writing majors could attract so many women? Dwayne certainly didn't.

College girls seemed to fawn over the guy in thick-rimmed glasses reading Hemingway and sipping a fat-free chai latte, so he dated as many girls as he could fit in his schedule.

Then, he met Lane.

Lane was a sophomore in his freshman writing class, a degree requirement she had intentionally forgotten about. She had brown curly hair and an affinity for her professor that made her untouchable. It was fate that she sat only one row in front of Dwayne, but she still refused to acknowledge his presence even when he made it blatantly apparent.

Lane wasn't impressed by the classic American literature he had posed on his desk, so he had to be resourceful. After all, girls loved him because he was a *creative*—a word he preferred as a noun rather than an adjective.

The semester pressed on, and Dwayne continued to have no luck until the last day of class. His time was running out, so he passed her a note that read, "Let me take you out for ice cream." Lane turned around, gave him a nod, and the rest is history. That is, until they got engaged.

Halfway into their yearlong engagement, Dwayne and Lane had one of their biggest fights yet. The added pressure of wedding planning has a special way of making something out of nothing. Small disagreements are easily blown out of proportion. A simple "I only got coffee for myself because I didn't know you wanted any" can turn into "Why did I choose to marry this person" in a matter of seconds. If you've been there, you know it's that powerful. If you haven't, God bless your soul.

This is what happened.

Dwayne is a freelance writer, and assumed he and Lane would write their own wedding vows. Would there ever be a better platform to show off his skills in front of his friends and family? Never. And the only problem he had was deciding how he wanted to write them. Would he write a poem or open with a dedication to his parents, a couple who showed him what it looked like to be happily married? Whatever he decided, he knew it would be epic, because "epic" is a word creatives like to use to describe anything mildly extraordinary.

Lane, on the other hand, hates public speaking and talking about her feelings in equal measure. She chose to work in a museum because, there, she spends her days surrounded by dead things and people who are headed in that direction. The idea of writing original vows didn't even cross her mind. As a matter of fact, she found comfort in the fact that the Lutheran Church had done her a service in that way. She'd grown up in the church attending Lutheran weddings, and they had their own set of traditional wedding vows that she could use. There was no reason to torture herself by writing her own.

Neither party was in the wrong, which made their disagreement all the more powerful. Combined with the potency of wedding planning pressure, the couple didn't stand a chance.

After an hour of angrily stating their cases, waiting for their turn to talk, and accusing each other of being selfish, they decided to take a break from the argument, which was going nowhere. Dwayne decided to call his mother to rally support for his position. She listened, took a breath, and cryptically responded, "Marriage is about compromise. Sounds like a chance to practice." It wasn't what he wanted to hear—but she was right.

It took three evenings and two bottles of wine, but they finally figured it out. Dwayne and Lane came to a compromise.

It was important to Dwayne to be able to write his own wedding vows, and that mattered to Lane. It was important to Lane not to add extra stress to her plate before the wedding, and that mattered to Dwayne. When you care about each other, there's always a compromise to be made.

The couple decided they would use a combination of original and traditional wedding vows.

Dwayne agreed to leave poetry and all of his other "fancy" techniques out of his vows so that Lane wouldn't feel added pressure about hers. The only poem she'd ever attempted to write was a Haiku, and that was before she'd known what "syllable" meant. Dwayne also agreed to incorporate the traditional Lutheran vows despite their being "overdone." Lane also asked him to stop saying "overdone," to which he reluctantly complied.

Lane agreed to write original wedding vows if Dwayne promised to help her with them. The idea still scared her, but love trumps fear. She also asked if they could have their vows completed at least three weeks before their wedding day so she would have time to practice the public speaking part of the process.

The couple toasted to their compromise with a third bottle of wine, and they eventually finished their vows with plenty of time to spare before their big day. Way to go, Dwayne and Lane.

Every couple has two personalities, two worldviews, and two sets of expectations, and that can make the beginning discussions of wedding vow writing complicated. Even if you and your partner agree on the basics, there are still details that need to be nailed down, and you'll likely have to compromise on a few things. You won't know what you're up against until you start the conversation.

First up, let's have the lessons you should learn from Dwayne and Lane about compromise, details, and planning.

Make sure all parties agree.

If you're like Dwayne, the idea of reading your intimate and romantic feelings out loud in front of an engaged audience feels energizing—but it was a nightmare for Lane. No matter where you're at on the spectrum, your partner could be on the other end. That's why it's important to start at the beginning by asking your partner how he or she feels about writing original vows.

If you're pushing to write your own vows, but your partner sounds hesitant, communicate why it's important to you. If your partner is asking you to write your vows, but you feel uncomfortable, explain your reasons. Your wedding day is about both of you, so you will likely have to meet somewhere in the middle.

It's not like the central theme of a wedding is joining two lives into one or anything.

If you're still not on the same page, you'll have to compromise. According to Ludwig Erhard, "A compromise is the art of dividing a cake in such a way that everyone believes he has the biggest piece."[3] At least everyone gets cake, right?

Talking openly about your desires and expectations like Dwayne and Lane did is the first step to compromise, and luckily, there aren't hard rules when it comes to wedding vow writing. It's your day, so you can literally do whatever you want. You want a short and sweet ceremony? Awesome. You want a string quartet and a cage full of doves released during your vows? More power to you. Everyone knows doves are the best.

Be sure to check with your officiant to see if there are any traditional vows that you need to include. These will vary by religious tradition, culture, and even officiant. You don't want to finish writing only to be surprised that you're required to add something else.

Discuss the details.

There are several details that need to be discussed after you decide to write your own wedding vows. If you come to a point where you disagree, get creative, and come up with a compromise like our friends Dwayne and Lane did. It's a much better alternative to killing each other. Here are a few questions you should discuss.

Do you want to write your vows together?

Some couples want to go through the process together while others would prefer to reveal them on their wedding day. If you or your partner have a hard time writing, especially on topics related to feelings and romance, it's probably best to work together to make the process smoother for both parties.

How long do you want your vows to be?

When you read your wedding vows out loud, they should be between one and five minutes long—two to three minutes is the sweet spot. Combined, your wedding vows should be no longer than ten minutes. If they're any longer, your guests will probably start thinking about the open bar instead of what you're saying.

Depending on your personalities, there will likely be some disparity in the length of your vows. Talkative people ramble, shy people rush, etc. And while this isn't a big deal, you won't want that gap to be too significant. A thirty-second difference is one thing, but if you talk for one minute and your partner talks for five, it might leave one of you feeling embarrassed or inadequate.

Do you want your vows to have similar structures?

This is an opportunity for your personality as a couple to shine through, so get as creative as you'd like. Maybe you both want to write poetry or use a few lines from the traditional Catholic wedding vows at the end. Do whatever feels the most comfortable for you and your partner. Lane asked Dwayne to keep his vows simple so that she could structure hers similarly, and that compromise gave her confidence.

Do you want to have a theme?

Themed vows have a unique way of personalizing the wedding ceremony. If you can't decide on a structure, but you're both musicians, you might choose a music theme and write songs for each other or include musical symbolism. And if you want to read a line or two of your vows in Klingon, no one can stop you. You're allowed to get as creative (or weird) with your theme as you'd like.

Set a due date.

If you're serious about writing your own vows, you and your partner need a little accountability. Your due date should be at least two weeks prior to your wedding. There are a few reasons for this.

First, you need to have plenty of time to rehearse your vows before your big day. Lane was uncomfortable with the idea of not having time to practice her vows, so their due date was three weeks out. Second, having a due date will prevent you from procrastinating until right before your wedding, which adds unnecessary stress to the writing process and your wedding day. And third, you'll have plenty of time to collaborate with your partner and make adjustments.

When you schedule a due date for your wedding vows, you should also make a plan for when you're going to work on them. You can take time in the evenings after work or right before bed, or you can work on the weekends. Whatever you decide, get it on paper, and hold each other to it.

Do your research

Chase & Grace

Grace's grandparents were the quintessential 1950s fairytale. If you've seen the movie Grease[4], they were kind of like that but with a lot less leather. They were gum-smacking, Elvis-loving high school sweethearts who remembered what life was like before television. And you can be sure that Grace, too, knew all about what life was like before television.

Her grandparents married shortly after their high school graduation, and the fairytale continued.

Their marriage survived wars, failed careers, and four children, so their advice was always practical...and sometimes wildly inappropriate. Or maybe sex advice from people over sixty-five just feels inappropriate.

One of Grace's grandmother's most practical pieces of advice for marital success was to "never argue when you're hungry," which explained the jumbo bag of honey roasted peanuts she always kept in her pocketbook. She also advised Grace to "stretch for five minutes every day so that, when you're old, you'll still be able to..." fill in the blank. Grace never had a hard time remembering that one; actually, she had a hard time forgetting it was ever said.

Her grandparents must have done something right. After over fifty years of marriage, they were still alive and kickin'. Needless to say, Grace wanted to be exactly like them, and after she met Chase, she finally had the chance.

Chase was thoughtful and adventurous, so the pair shared plenty of fun memories together. Like the time they watched YouTube videos of teacup piglets, and Chase decided to buy one on Craig's List. He thought the breeder might be shady because of the watermarked stock images in his ad, but it didn't matter. His prices were the bomb. Unsurprisingly, the young couple learned their pig wasn't a teacup when it weighed 50 pounds six months later, so they sold him to a local farm. But for six whole months, they enjoyed being a two-person, one-pig family.

Grace's grandparents approved of Chase, a prerequisite for her life partner. So, after he proposed, they were the first people they told. Her grandparents were thrilled.

With only four months until the wedding, Chase and Grace decided to write their own wedding vows. It was a mutual decision that resulted in a less-than-mutual panic. Grace needed the ceremony to be perfect, and there's nothing a perfectionist likes more than research and preparation.

To prepare for vow writing, the couple planned a date night that involved tacos and a whole lot of communication. Nothing says "let's communicate" like a date night in. And apparently, nothing says "let's write some vows" like tacos. What can't tacos do?

The couple talked about where they had been and where they were headed, and they divvied up the talking points. They browsed the internet for wedding vow examples and printed out their favorites. They also wanted to pay tribute to Grace's grandparents, a marriage that would serve as an example for the rest of their lives. They even included a piece of her grandmother's wildly inappropriate advice. By the end of the night, they had settled on a plan.

Their preparation paid off in the end. There wasn't a dry eye at the ceremony when they honored Grace's grandparents. Nothing makes a wedding crowd cry faster than living proof that love is the most powerful force in the world. Right on, Chase and Grace.

It's hard to write vows that will make everyone cry. The good news is that, if you and your partner put in the work up front and do your research, you can simplify the process exponentially. If you and your partner reminisce about your past and dream about your future like Chase and Grace did over tacos, you can cover a lot of ground. And by discussing your role models and reading through wedding vow examples, you get a better idea of what kind of marriage you want to have and how to express that in writing.

Do your research like Chase and Grace, and get prepared by following in their footsteps in the following ways.

Plan a date.

You've decided with your partner to write your own wedding vows, discussed the details, and even set a due date for yourselves. Now, it's time to do a little research. The first thing you'll need to do?

Plan a date to dive into your story.

There will be no literal diving, so no floaties will be necessary. Instead, you and your partner will dive into your relationship, which is way more fun than literal diving anyway. Unless you're diving for treasure; then you're having the most fun by far.

Set aside one evening for you and your fiancé, preferably in a quiet, private place where you can talk, laugh, and take notes. Your job that night will include taking a walk down memory lane, discussing the current state of your relationship, and dreaming about the future together. This should be as fun as it sounds.

First, you'll want to discuss the journey that brought you where you are today. This is your chance to revisit your favorite memories and to laugh way more than usual. Did you ever buy a teacup piglet like Chase and Grace? No? That's too bad.

You'll want to talk about your first date, how you met, and all of the things that make your relationship unique. As you're discussing these things, take notes so that you can remember the funniest moments and your favorite memories. These are the types of things you'll want to include in your wedding vows.

Next, it's time to have a little DTR. Thankfully, "Define the Relationship" doesn't cause a fraction of the anxiety it did during your dating years when there was a 50/50 chance your "I love you" would be followed with "It's not you, it's me." Now that you're engaged, you and your partner can discuss your relationship without feeling like you're going to vomit.

You'll want to discuss topics like how you make each other better, how you handle conflict, and what your favorite things are about your relationship. Explore the reasons you chose to marry this person. Keep notes as you go, and enjoy the romantic ambience such a discussion can create.

Finally, you'll want to talk about your future. Your wedding day is the first day of the rest of your life together, so it's wise to plan for it the best you can. Talk about how you'll handle successes and failures and how you can handle conflict better in the future. List out the values that you share and what that will mean for future decisions. For example, if you both value family, you'll prioritize time at home over time working at the office.

Refer to the guide in your Wedding Vow Journal for questions and topics to go over with your partner.

Discuss your role models.

It takes years to learn how to be married—like, a lot of them. If you're someone who expects to walk down the aisle and become an expert, you'll have a lot of explaining to do when you find yourself arguing with your partner about ramen flavors at the supermarket. Rather than assuming you've got what it takes to have a vibrant, healthy marriage, have a little humility, and trust the ones who have gone before you.

It's perfectly normal for newlyweds to spend the majority of their time wondering what the hell is going on.

Hopefully, there are married couples in your life that have influenced you positively like Grace's grandparents. Maybe your parents disagree gracefully, or your best friend treats his wife like a queen. Whoever it is, their role in your life is important, because they show you what marriage actually looks like. If you're aiming for a perfect happily ever after, you'll be sorely disappointed.

Is there a couple that you respect enough to imitate in your marriage? Discuss the things you admire about them with your partner. What parts of their relationship do you respect the most? How can you apply what you've learned from them to your relationship now?

By answering these questions, you're creating benchmarks and discovering the areas that you'll need to work on. You'll also be prepared when you're writing your vows because you know what you're shooting for, and you've learned tangible ways to get there.

Borrow from the pros.

You don't have to go it alone. It's perfectly acceptable to browse the internet for examples like Chase and Grace did or to borrow ideas from professional writers. You can even imitate another set of vows that you love. Austin Kleon suggests in his book *Steal Like an Artist* that all art is stolen to some degree, so don't beat yourself up if you decide to do a little stealing yourself.[5]

Here are a few examples for you to borrow or learn from.

Romantic Vows.

I knew you were the one I wanted to share my life with from the moment I saw you. I'm captivated by your beauty, a beauty that runs to the depths of your soul. You inspire me every day to be the best version of myself that I can be. I will love you forever, and I promise to honor and cherish you as I share the rest of my days with you. I promise to choose selflessness every day. You are my world and my priority, and I promise to treat you like you are. Everything that I have, everything that I own, everything that I am, I give to you today. You are my other half, the one I've been waiting for my whole life.

Today, our lives are joining together, two paths merging to form one journey. We are going to build a home together where love is valued above all else, love for each other and for others. We'll teach our children how to believe in themselves and how to serve those in need, and we'll grow a family that will change the world. I vow to protect and honor our marriage every day for the rest of my life. And on the days when I feel like I have nothing left to offer, I promise to love you still. Today, I take you, [name], to be my lawfully wedded husband/wife.

Funny Vows.

Wife: I, [your name], take you, studly bearded one, to be my husband, my partner, my best friend. From this day forward, I will support your dreams, even when they include time travel. And I will keep my sass to a minimum, especially on game days. When you're upset, I promise to let you be the little spoon. And when you're being difficult, I will resist the urge to lock you outside until you're ready to play nice. In the presence of our family and friends, I solemnly vow to be your wife and partner in crime…crimes I won't mention now so that our family and friends won't have to lie in court. I promise, from this day forward, to work hard to be the wife you've always dreamed of and to love you as selflessly as I know how.

Husband: Today, I vow to be your lawfully wedded husband, even when you ask me to repeat myself for the third time because you weren't paying attention. I promise to protect, cherish, and honor you, even when you've spent the evening crying about a movie you shouldn't have watched in the first place. I adore everything about you, especially your laugh and your little meatball toes. I will be with you in the valleys and on the mountaintops, and when life gives you lemons, I'll add liquor to your lemonade. And when your old cat finally dies, I promise to hold you until you're ready for me to let go. Even when I'm not in the same room, I promise that your soul will never be lonely again. You are my cherished treasure, and from this day forward, you are my priority, even when the Cowboys make it to the playoffs.

Music-Themed Vows.

[Name], when I met you, my life changed keys. On our first date, when I learned you loved The Beatles, I had a feeling you were the one. Things were never the same after we fell in love, and I knew I had to be with you forever. You are the one person in this world that makes me want to go from solo to duo. You're the one I've been waiting for. I promise to sit with you in silence when I don't have all the answers, and I promise to stay put even when I want to run away. We're a two-piece ensemble, and I look forward to creating beautiful music with you for the rest of our lives. From this day forward, I take you, [name], as my lawfully wedded husband/wife.

Adventure-Themed Vows.

Today, we begin the adventure of a lifetime. I've found my soulmate, and I can't wait to begin a new journey together. I promise to stay by your side through the highs and the lows of life. When the tide rises, and we feel like we're drowning, I promise to stretch myself so that I can hold out my hand for you to grab. When the sun rises, and all is well in the world, I promise to celebrate with you and hold you tight. The world is full of distractions, but I promise to pursue you above all else for the rest of my life. I promise to take chances with you and to create a life full of adventure. In sickness and in health, for richer or for poorer, you will never have to walk alone again.

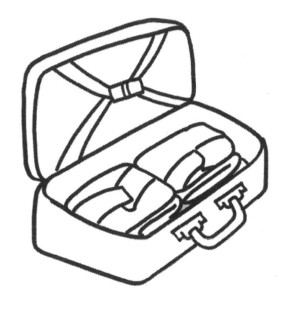

Final preparations

Leo & Cleo

Everyone knew they would get married one day. Leo and Cleo were high school sweethearts, and their relationship never got complicated the way 99.9% of high school relationships do. Even when Cleo decided to go to a college that was 150 miles away, their commitment remained strong.

During Cleo's junior year, the couple got engaged and planned to get married after her graduation. Their engagement lasted for a year and a half. They had plenty of time to sort out their wedding plans, so their stress levels were low even as their wedding day approached.

Leo and Cleo decided to write their own vows long before their big day, a natural decision for the couple. Cleo worked as a journalist, so she spent time writing every day of her life. Leo, though an inexperienced writer, had full confidence that he could find the right words to say to the woman he'd loved for well over five years.

But Cleo didn't intend to procrastinate as badly as she did.

The night before the wedding, Cleo still had her wedding vows to write—but she wasn't that worried about it. She had an idea of what she wanted to say, and the couple had decided that their vows would only be a total of five minutes long. What professional couldn't churn out two and a half minutes with ease? Plus, her wedding didn't start until five o'clock, and she was an early riser.

However, a combination of nerves, vivid dreams, and whiskey from the night before caused Cleo to wake up later than usual. She rushed to breakfast only to find that she was the last one up. Rather than fussing that no one had awakened her, she gleefully joined her party.

After filling up on chocolate chip pancakes, Cleo retreated to her bridal suite to finally begin writing her vows. She explained her need for privacy, and her bridesmaids understood. They even guarded the door so that no person or problem could interrupt.

Cleo pulled out a blank notebook and began writing. The words were coming easily. She was in the groove. After a couple of minutes, she was three sentences into her vows.

Then, her pen ran out of ink.

"Really, pen? What is your problem?" Cleo whispered under her breath. If pens could talk, it probably would've scolded her for procrastinating. Then, it would've told her to keep calm and stay focused because, apparently, pens have a balanced approach to conflict. Unfortunately, though, pens can't talk, so she threw it across the room. She searched for a replacement, growing more frustrated with every passing minute.

After a replacement was found, Cleo started a bulleted list to organize her ideas before she continued. She was convinced that she was missing something important. She had never been married before, so how would she know if she'd covered all of her bases? Maybe there was some secret language that all happily married people were aware of. Maybe there was a club. She had no idea, so she summoned her parents to her guarded bridal quarters to ask for their advice. They made it through security unscathed.

As soon as they walked in, Cleo knew something was wrong.

Her parents had spent the morning in tears about the marriage of their baby girl, and the tears were still coming. They'd had plenty of time to prepare for this day, but that didn't make a difference. Instead of receiving their sage advice, Cleo spent the next hour consoling and reminiscing with her parents. Finally, though, her parents reviewed her bullet points and reminded her to include a line or two about the future she hoped she and Leo would build together. Cleo added the suggestion to her list, and, as tearfully as her parents had entered, they left.

Emotional from the conversation, Cleo continued on her vows. She was starting to get tense, because she couldn't get back into the groove. She needed some inspiration to get her train of thought back on track, and since sneaking away to make out with Leo wasn't an option, she decided to watch wedding vow videos online for half an hour. That did the trick.

Then, there was a knock on the door.

She was making some really good progress when her hair and makeup artist showed up an hour early. "I didn't think two hours would be enough time, so I came early. I hope that's ok," the artist said as she entered the room.

What fresh hell is this, Cleo thought.

So there she was, getting her hair and makeup done with a notebook in her hand. It's hard to think romantic thoughts when hair is being plucked from your face, and it's even harder to write those thoughts down when you're being repeatedly asked to shut your eyes. At this point, there was no groove in sight.

Cleo wanted to add a creative element to her vows, and she was running out of time. So she came up with a win–win solution. She decided to open her vows with a quote from her favorite author, Elizabeth Gilbert.

"People think a soulmate is your perfect fit, and that's what everyone wants. But a true soulmate is a mirror, the person who shows you everything that is holding you back, the person who brings you to your own attention so you can change your life."[6]

Cleo finished her vows with an hour to spare. She handed her notebook over to her maid of honor, cursing it under her breath. She had learned a valuable lesson that, fortunately, she would never be able to apply. She preached it to every bride-to-be who would listen: Don't wait until the last minute to write your wedding vows. Your pen will run out of ink, your parents will cry, and it's just not worth it.

Despite the day's rocky start, the couple exchanged vows and had a beautiful ceremony. And even though there were a few things she would've changed, Cleo was proud of her work. Congrats, Leo and Cleo.

Vow writing requires time and focus, even for the most experienced writers. Anything can happen during those final days before your wedding, and the stress of procrastinating isn't worth it during such an important time. As a rule of thumb, aim to finish your vows at least two weeks before your wedding day.

And while the obvious moral of Leo and Cleo's story is that you shouldn't procrastinate, there are a few other lessons about final prep that their story can teach us.

Get advice.

There's no way for you to be fully prepared for marriage. Marriage is unlike any experience or relationship you've ever had. That's why Cleo decided to ask her parents for advice on her wedding vows, even if she did do it at the last minute.

If you want your vows to reflect the realities of marriage, it's wise to get advice from a marriage veteran in your life. If you've never been married, then your idea of marriage is likely incomplete or idealized. And nothing is less inspiring (and more nauseating) than two never-marrieds rambling on and on about the perfect marriage they're going to have.

Marriage veterans bravely forged a path for you to follow, and really, they deserve recognition for choosing marriage in the first place. Subjecting yourself to a lifetime of growth and living selflessly for the sake of love and family isn't a small thing. They've experienced the realities of marriage, and those realities probably fall short of "happily ever after."

Conduct a short interview with a couple that you deeply respect with a healthy marriage. It could be your parents, your future in-laws, or even your grandparents. If there isn't a couple in your family to reach out to, begin thinking about your friends and mentors.

After you've chosen a couple, ask them to sit down with you. Your goal during this interview will be to learn about the important parts of marriage so that you can address them in your vows. Here are a few example questions for you to ask them:

1. What do you wish you knew before you got married?

2. What roadblocks or struggles should we expect?

3. What would you tell us to remember as newlyweds?

4. What is your best marriage advice?

Record their answers, and highlight the parts that stick out to you. This information will help you write meaningful vows that are relevant and inspiring. You'll find a complete list of questions for your interview in your Wedding Vow Journal.

Get creative.

If you're the creative type, then you've already had plenty of opportunities to express that creativity during your wedding planning. Thankfully, the fun doesn't have to stop with the custom cocktails and the stack of donuts that'll act as your wedding cake. It's time to add a little flair to your wedding vows.

Keep in mind that whatever you do should mirror your personality in an obvious way. If you're shy, bursting into song for the sake of being creative isn't recommended, especially if you sing like William Hung. Cleo chose to quote her favorite author, Elizabeth Gilbert, which also reflected the fact that she's a writer herself.

Add a few jokes. Do an impression. Speak in multiple languages. Tell a story. Quote your favorite artist or philosopher—like Taylor Swift: "I knew you were trouble when you walked in...."[7]

There are countless ways to get creative with your vow writing. If you really want to add a unique element, but you're not sure what to do, take a few minutes to think about what you love the most. It could be an activity, a person, a form of entertainment, etc. Then come up with a creative way to incorporate it.

Excessive profanity, sexual content, and nudity are not recommended, no matter how creative or "you" they might be.

Get inspired.

If you've felt a little uninspired by the process so far, you're not alone. Just like any worthwhile endeavor, writing your own wedding vows takes time and dedication. It's not easy, especially when you're doing it right, but the payoff will last a lifetime. These are the most significant words you'll ever say, even more significant than the time you told your mom you couldn't tell her the "right" moment for her to discuss what she learned in sex therapy with you...because that moment is never.

Cleo struggled for inspiration as she rushed to complete her vows, so she took half an hour to watch other couples say theirs online. Taking your time is a big part of staying motivated. There's nothing less inspiring than having to finish your vows in one quick, high-pressure session like Cleo did. But when the inspiration wears off (and it will), don't fret, because inspiration is everywhere.

What are your favorite romantic comedies or dramas? Do you have a favorite love song or a song that reminds you of your relationship? Have you ever read love poetry? Starting your writing sessions with a romantic element is the perfect way to get into the right mindset.

Choose a structure

Dan & Anne

Dan and Anne were just the people you would expect to write their own wedding vows.

Dan was an art teacher at a private elementary school. He was the kind of man who could spend every day in a room full of children over whom he had no real control. The noise, the mess, and even the lack of clarity in curriculum didn't bother Dan. He was a rare breed, and he didn't just tolerate his job...he loved it.

Anne was a singer-songwriter. She taught guitar lessons and had a regular gig at the coffee shop down the street. She hummed various melodies from the moment she woke up until she fell asleep at night, a trait she claimed was proof that she didn't choose music; music chose her. Dreams of fame were never her driving force. In fact, Anne believed fame to be toxic after her second cousin was cast in a series of mayo commercials and stopped returning her calls.

Dan and Anne were content, and the life they built together was a reflection of that. They painted bright colors on their walls and squeezed fresh citrus juices every week. Their jobs, hobbies, and friendships were as unique as they were. They even had a bulldog named Peanut.

Originality was kind of their thing.

After their engagement, writing original wedding vows was sort of like an unspoken agreement. Dan and Anne had nonverbal communication skills that bordered on telepathy, a likely result of the eight years they'd dated. Sure, eight years sounds like a long time, but it's only long if you're rushing through life—or at least that's what Dan would say anytime he was asked about it. He didn't want to sound noncommittal.

One month before their wedding, Dan and Anne sat down together to write their vows. One month would sound like procrastination to anyone else, but the couple claimed they saved the best for last. Plus, they assumed it wouldn't take them long. After eight years together, they had plenty of raw material to work with.

That first Saturday afternoon, Dan and Anne sat down to begin writing. She wanted to begin with a song, and he wanted to write call-and-response vows like he had seen a friend and fellow art teacher do at his wedding the year before. Right away, the couple realized the process wouldn't be as easy as they'd thought.

They didn't lack content. They had plenty of experience and original ideas, and they borrowed from past weddings they'd attended. The problem was figuring out how to structure them all. But on their third try, they nailed it. Here's what they came up with:

> (4 mins) Love song written by Anne.

> (5 mins) First date and first kiss story told by Dan.

> (3 mins) Proposal story told by Anne.

> (3 mins) Vows written by Dan.

> (3 mins) Vows written by Anne.

> (5 mins) Call-and-response vows written by Dan.

Dan and Anne were pleased. They were able to include all of their best ideas in a structure that flowed well. This draft was true to their personalities, both as individuals and as a couple.

The only problem was that twenty-three minutes seemed long. But surely twenty-three minutes of pure romance would captivate a crowd, not overwhelm or bore them. Surely their guests would enjoy their hour-long ceremony, even though Dan and Anne hated attending long wedding ceremonies themselves. But they weren't sure, so they asked around.

The feedback was unanimous: twenty-three minutes was *way* too long for wedding vows.

So after many hours, tears, and disagreements, they pared down the list. They kept and shortened the parts that meant the most to them, and, even though it was a hard process, they were pleased with the result. Their new structure looked like this:

> (3 mins) Love song written by Anne.

> (2 mins) First date story told by Dan.

> (2 mins) Vows written by Anne.

> (2 mins) Call-and-response vows written by Dan.

With less to do, Dan and Anne were able to focus their energy on making their vows more meaningful and mind-blowing. They were also pleased that they didn't have to sacrifice originality with their new structure. And at nine minutes long, they eliminated their guests' risk of death by boredom. Great job, Dan and Anne.

When you're deciding on a structure for your vows, your first focus should be your partner and your new marriage. That's what this whole thing is about, isn't it? It should also reflect your personalities and complement the flow of your ceremony. If you choose a structure that's too long or random or that affects your wedding guests or your ceremony flow in a negative way, reconsider it like Dan and Anne did. You'll probably come up with something you like better.

It's time to choose a structure. Here are the lessons you can learn from Dan and Anne's story.

Know your options.

You have to think big picture about your wedding vows. Dan and Anne got caught up in the details at first, but eventually, they figured it out. Your goal should be to choose a simple structure that fits well into your ceremony and mirrors your personalities. If you're not sure where to start, review the most commonly used structures below.

Combine traditional and original vows.

If you're torn between the originality of writing your own vows and the romance and history of reciting traditional vows, don't shed another tear about it. This is now one of the most common structures for marrying couples. Here is an example of this structure:

"When you came into my life, you lit up my world. I can see clearly for the first time, and I never want to live another day without you. I promise to honor and cherish you for the rest of our lives. Today, I take you as my wife, to have and to hold from this day forward, for better, for worse, for richer, for poorer, in sickness and health, until death do us part."

Read the same original vows.

This structure might sound uninspired, but keep in mind that this is how traditional vows have been structured for centuries. During the ceremony, the couple would recite the same prewritten vows to one another. So if you decide to write vows that both you and your fiancé will read during the ceremony, you'll be in good company.

Write complementary vows.

This structure is perfect if you want to get creative, and there are several different ways to do it. You and your partner could write separate, original vows and then recite the same closing statements. Or you could write vows that complement each other. For example, "I take you as my wife, to have and to hold, and to drag outside on sunny days" complements the line, "I take you to be my husband, to have and to hold, and to smother with sunscreen when you forget how badly your fair skin burns on sunny days."

Another option is to discuss different parts of your relationship in your half of the vows. Perhaps you talk about how you met, and your partner talks about your first date, or you discuss your individual roles in eliminating any spider that might (will) invade your home. If you choose to write complementary vows, you'll have lot of room for creativity and personalization.

Call-and-response vows.

This is the least traditional structure of all, but this back-and-forth style has grown in popularity over recent years. It requires cooperation from both parties, making it more difficult to complete. One partner reads a line that's quickly followed by the other's response related to that line, and this continues for the duration of the vows. Think "Señorita"[8] by Justin Timberlake....

Guys sing… It feels like something's heating up, can I leave with you?

Ladies… I don't know what I'm thinking 'bout, really leaving with you.

The key to writing successful call-and-response vows is to make sure every line flows together. One partner might say, "You are the strength I needed to pursue my dreams," followed by the other saying, "You give me strength to be the person I want to be."

You have full creative liberty with your wedding vows. If you want to include each of these structures in a small way, have at it. If you want to do something totally out of the box, like write your partner a song, then go get 'em. These structures are meant to guide you toward your goal, not confine you to creative boundaries.

Let your personality shine through.

Marriage is about individuals joining their lives together and creating a new union. Every couple has two personalities, two sets of goals, and two opinions about Cheetos (crunchy or puffy?). After you get married, you don't just have your identity as an individual; you have an identity as a couple. Who you are and what you value as a unit is just as important.

You should emphasize your individual personalities *and* your identity as a couple in your wedding vows. Dan and Anne did a really good job with this. It isn't a one-size-fits-all process, so you may have to make adjustments along the way.

Take a moment to think about the traits and qualities that make you who you are, and then brainstorm a few creative ways to apply what you learned.

If you're a songwriter, write a song.

If you're funny, add humor.

If you're an engineer, use metaphors from your field.

If you're a poet, write a poem.

If you're into math, quote Euclid.

Seriously, the possibilities are endless. Get deep, get silly, and personalize your vows with the structure you choose. A little thought and creativity can go a long way.

Don't worry about being too original.

Yes, reinforce your identity as an individual and as a couple in your wedding vows, but don't stress about being too original. Even Dan and Anne borrowed ideas from previous weddings they had attended. The unique lines you write will personalize your vows, but borrowing from traditional versions and others is a good tool.

Here are examples for you to borrow and learn from for each of the wedding vow structures.

Example: Combine traditional and original vows.

You are my perfect match. I never knew what I needed in a life partner, but that changed after you taught me what it meant to love someone. You blow me away every day with how well you love me. I'm forever grateful for the encourager, adventurer, and lover you so naturally are. In the name of God, I, [name], take you, [partner's name], to be my wife/husband, to have and to hold from this day forward, for better, for worse, for richer, for poorer, in sickness and in health, to love and to cherish, until we are parted by death. This is my solemn vow."

Example: The same original vows.

[Partner's name], I want you exactly as you are. Loving you has been the greatest honor of my life. From this day forward, I promise to choose compromise over pride. I promise to celebrate your wins and hold you close through your losses. I will be your biggest supporter and advocate. You are my best friend. Today, I take you, [partner's name], as my lawfully wedded husband/wife.

Example: Complementary vows.

Husband: I, [name], take you, [partner's name], to be my wife. I love all of the things I know about you, and I trust that I'll love what I discover. When things get hard, I promise to swallow my pride, carry my part of the burden, and walk beside you every day. I promise to support your dreams and share your goals. Our future is so bright. I can't wait to start a family with you. You are my motivation, my first priority, and the love of my life. I am yours from this day forward.

Wife: I, [name], take you, [partner's name], to be my husband. Every part of me is in love with every part of you, even the parts I don't know yet. When the world isn't kind to us, and we're overcome by struggles, I promise to support you the best way I know how. I promise to share in all of your dreams and to encourage you when you feel like giving up. I look forward to the beautiful life we're going to build together. You are going to be the best dad. You are my strength, my inspiration, and the love of my life. I am devoted to you from this day forward.

Example: Call and response vows.

Husband: [Partner's name], I've known since we met that I wanted to make you my wife. Your smile overwhelmed me, and you spoke with such grace and kindness. You are unlike any other person I've ever known.

Wife: [Partner's name], I knew I wanted to be with you forever after our third date. Watching you handle your struggles with integrity and a willingness to learn inspired me to look inward. You make me want to be a better person.

Husband: You teach me something new and beautiful every day. The lens through which you see your life is so full of joy, it's contagious.

Wife: You have a way of making me feel seen and loved like I've never experienced. Your life is a reflection of your courage, determination, and authenticity.

Husband: I promise to stand by your side when we experience the many trials of life. And when those trials involve our marriage, I promise to be humble and to always be willing to learn and grow.

Wife: I promise I won't run away when things get hard; instead, I'll support and honor you. I also promise to own my mistakes, even when I'm feeling stubborn, and to handle yours with grace.

Husband: You are mine, to have and to hold, for better or for worse, for richer or for poorer. Anywhere that life takes us, I promise that I'm not going anywhere.

Wife: You are mine, in sickness and in health, to love and to cherish, until we are parted by death. I promise to love you the best way I know how.

Husband: Today, I take you, [partner's name], as my wife.

Wife: Today, I take you, [partner's name], as my husband.

Set your tone

Ben & Ren

Ben met Ren at a birthday party. Ben had been asking a mutual friend to introduce him to Ren for months, and this party was his opportunity. After they met, the mutual friend told Ren that she wasn't being set up with Ben. Rather, their chemistry was a result of fate. The couple went on their first date the next day.

Their mutual friend would later admit to the matchmaking scheme. Ren preferred it to fate anyway.

Matchmaking is a paradox: Everyone wants to be set up, but no one wants to admit they toyed with fate. You think "I was lonely and tired of searching for love by myself, so a friend helped me out" is less romantic than "The stars aligned, and the gods of passion crossed our paths, and we happened upon one another on a midnight stroll." But it's not, especially in the 21st century when late night strolls imply that you might be a streetwalker, a less than virtuous profession.

Ben was an energetic, outgoing marketing executive who loved the beach and spending time with his family. Ren was a nurse by trade and a caretaker by nature. She loved lowbrow reality television and shared Ben's affection for the water.

Seven months after they met, Ben got down on one knee in the sand and proposed. The two fell quickly, but no one in their lives could deny how right it was. And since Ben was being relocated for work, they decided to get married before they moved.

That gave them three months to plan a wedding.

There were hundreds of details that had to be settled before the couple could even think about their wedding vows, so when the time came, they were exhausted. Ben and Ren decided that their vows would be half original and half traditional to minimize the workload. They also wanted to have a short ceremony, so they were going to keep their vows to less than three minutes each.

Ren's mother advised the couple to spend time in thought about the tone they would set with their vows. The concern was fresh in her mind; she had attended a wedding the week before where the bride and groom had written vows that felt more like stand-up comedy. The humor felt displaced and insincere in an otherwise intense and solemn ceremony.

Ben and Ren disregarded the advice as overkill. They proceeded to write their wedding vows as quickly as they could in order to move on to the next item on their to-do list. When they were finished, they got together to read their final versions.

Ben filled his vows with so many clichés that they sounded ironic. "You're the sun in my sky, my wings in flight, my partner in crime...." The unintentional rhyming didn't help.

Ren used language that depicted her as obsessive and a little bit terrifying: "I don't know how I lived without you. You're the air I breathe and the only thing I need. I can't wait to share every day with you and watch you while you sleep." Yikes.

Their vows didn't reflect their personalities—or really anything remotely related to their wedding day. Sure, there were some good ideas in the mix, but they had to start over. Perhaps tone merited a discussion after all.

Ben and Ren decided to work together to maximize the small amount of time they had left before the wedding. They discussed their options for tone and made a decision that mirrored their relationship. They wanted to write vows that were fun and light-hearted but passionate.

The couple would write in a conversational manner and emphasize their rich experiences together. Their vows would overflow with romance, and they would add a pinch of humor. It was no secret that their relationship had progressed quickly, and they believed it was because there's nothing complicated about finding your soul mate.

Ben and Ren didn't want to eliminate the most relevant clichés, so they decided to remix them.

"Love at first sight" became "The first time I saw you at the party, you looked familiar in a way I couldn't describe. It was like our souls had already met."

"You are my world" became "You've given my life greater purpose. My love for you has made me more selfless and kind. It's changed the way I process the world."

"I love you more than anything" became "You are my first priority, the love of my life. When other things battle for my attention, I promise you'll always be my number one."

In the end, Ben and Ren wrote powerful wedding vows that mirrored who they were as a couple. By refocusing around tone, they were able to write authentically and communicate effectively. That's the way it's done, Ben and Ren.

If you're not in a creative profession, then taking time to think about the tone of your wedding vows isn't intuitive. As a matter of fact, your thoughts on tone have probably been pretty limited up until this point.... Tone is what you want your muscles to have, right? But discussing and deciding on a tone before you begin writing will save you a ton of time and mental energy, which you'll need for the other treacherous parts of wedding planning (guest list, anyone?), and it'll ensure that you and your partner are on the same page.

Set the tone for your vows with these lessons from Ben and Ren about options, personalization, and clichés.

Pick a tone.

Setting the tone for your wedding vows can be tricky. If you're anything like Ben and Ren, you assume a solid structure is all you need, and you rewrite your vows until you get it right. But with the right tone, you can prevent unnecessary rewrites.

Some couples decide to be comedians at the altar while others prefer to pour out their hearts. No way is better than the other, but you will want to consider the tone of your ceremony before you decide. Your vows should flow seamlessly with the other elements, which means you probably shouldn't follow up a traditional Roman Catholic prayer with lyrics from Kanye. Unless you regularly quote Kanye at inappropriate times; then it's fine.

If you're wondering what it looks like to set the tone for your vows, check out the examples below:

"I grew up in a religious home, so I want my vows to have a religious theme but also feel compelling and authentic."

"I'm going to write honest vows that are full of heartfelt lines, but I want them to be packed with imagery and have a whimsical feel to reflect my creative personality."

"Since my fiancé and I love to laugh together, I want to write humorous vows that still have a deep, romantic feel."

Don't overcomplicate this part. As you can tell from the examples above, the tone you set should be two things: simple and true to who you are.

Make it personal.

Sometimes, getting personal can be uncomfortable. Like when an acquaintance overshares about a wild night out or when you're asked to present "one interesting fact about yourself" during an icebreaker. Fortunately for you, your wedding guests already know you and/or your partner, so the discomfort should be kept to a minimum...unless your grandmother calls your fiancé by your ex-boyfriend's name.

Your vows should be personal, and choosing a tone is one of the best ways to personalize them. This isn't the time to write something that's out of character or that might give your partner second thoughts about the union...like Ren's unintentionally obsessive and terrifying vows. Scaring your soon-to-be-spouse is definitely a no-no.

If you're funny, incorporate humor. If you're religious, talk about your faith. If you're a hopeless romantic, pretend you're in a Katherine Heigl movie. Your tone can go a hundred different ways, so be sure to make it personal.

Remember that clichés are faux pas.

You are my knight in shining armor. You had me at hello. Love is blind. I get butterflies when you're around. Why buy the cow when you can get the milk for free?

You see where this is headed.

Clichés are the tired phrases about love that you've heard a thousand times at weddings, in songs, and probably from your ex. Not only do they give your vows a generic feel, but they have a way of making your love sound immature and juvenile. Even when they're true, they're hard to take seriously, because they're so overdone.

This doesn't mean that you should ignore the obvious truths about your relationship just because they sound like a well-known saying. It does mean that you should rework your words to sound more original when possible. Remixing relevant clichés, like Ben and Ren did, is a perfect alternative.

For example, when you tell your partner he or she is beautiful inside and out, you're saying that you admire his or her looks in addition to personality, spirituality, etc. So instead of using a cliché, try saying something like, "Your gorgeous smile is only a reflection of the joy that radiates from your heart" or "I could stare at you all day long, but the best part of being with you is that I get to share my life with the most beautiful soul I've ever met."

If there's a saying that speaks beautifully to where you are as a couple, you should include it. The goal is to avoid overdoing it with clichés, not to obsess about being completely original.

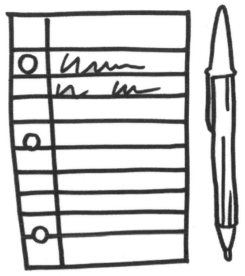

Put pen to paper

Sam & Pam

Sam and Pam were well loved by their coworkers, so when they started dating, no one said a word to management. Watching them fall in love was entertainment for everyone at the office.

A few weeks into their romance, a jealous coworker casually outed them in a meeting. Their supervisor pretended she didn't hear the comment. Their job performance hadn't suffered, and they were darling as hell.

Less than a year later, Sam proposed on a Friday afternoon in front of the people who had watched their love story unfold.

During their first conversation about wedding plans, Sam tried to convince Pam that they needed to write original wedding vows. She was hesitant and said, "People like me don't do things like that." When Sam asked her what she meant by "people like me" and "things like that," she skillfully avoided the question and changed the subject.

Despite her hesitancy, she agreed to give it a try, but she had two stipulations. First, if she didn't like what she wrote when it was all said and done, they would cut them out of the ceremony. Second, they would be methodical about the vow-writing process and plan ahead so that it added no extra stress to their wedding planning.

Sam complied. He wasn't sure if he was Ursula or Ariel in this contract scenario or if he would come to regret the agreement. He also wasn't sure why he was thinking about the situation in *Little Mermaid* terms.[9]

Sam and Pam got together on a Sunday afternoon less than two weeks after their engagement to begin talking about the vows they were going to write. They had two pens, two sheets of paper, and two very different sets of expectations. They weren't sure how to get started, so they decided to make a few lists.

The first was a list of all of their favorite things about each other. The second was all about their favorite memories. The third list included all of the ways they supported each other as a couple, and that list revealed that Sam and Pam didn't have the most run-of-the-mill relationship. Here are a few things from that list:

1. Sam keeps Pam's office stocked with fresh, seasonal flowers because they make her happy every time she sees them. He replaces them every 4–5 days, and it costs him approximately $90/month.

2. Pam keeps a tub of microwaveable fondue chocolate in her pantry for Sam because he loves to dip his dessert (and occasionally his dinner) in it. While he's dipping, he usually asks, "Why fon-don't when you can fon-do?"—a question so genuine that she can't help but keep the fondue flowing.

3. Sam and Pam share an appreciation for bubble baths as the most enjoyable form of bathing and the most effective form of relaxing. When either of them has a bad day, the other knows to run a bath. Lavender-scented bubbles, bath salts, rubber ducks, and even bath snacks are all acceptable (and appreciated) additions.

Their lists were helping them see their relationship more clearly, but they agreed there was still something missing. Sam and Pam decided to dive deeper and make a list of things about their relationship that were further beneath the surface. Here are a few things from the list:

1. They both knew shortly after they met that their connection went deeper than work discussions and their taste in music.

2. Pam found it hard to describe her relationship to her close friends and family members because of how natural it feels.

3. Sam realized he believes in soul mates, a concept he always assumed was made up until he met Pam.

This final list brought greater clarity. The couple felt energized by their lists because they were producing great content for their vows. Pam's confidence in the process was rising, and she was pleasantly surprised to learn that "people like her" are more than capable of writing their own vows…or, as she might say, "things like that."

If their first step was gathering great content for their vows, the next step was getting organized. The couple decided they would make an outline to organize everything they had. Pam had learned how to draw up an outline in her college English classes, so it was her suggestion.

Sam and Pam wanted to write complementary vows, so they decided to both use the same outline. It was simple, but it was all the structure they needed to get started.

Sam & Pam's Outline

1. The Reasons Why I Love You
   A. The things that I love about you
   B. The qualities that I respect
   C. The traits that I admire

2. The Evidence That You're Perfect For Me
   A. The things that make our relationship unique
   B. The ways you support me
   C. The reasons you make me want to be a better person

3. The Promises I Want To Make
   A. The ways I promise to treat you
   B. The part I'll be playing in creating a healthy marriage
   C. The ways I'll work on becoming the best version of myself for you

All of the list-making and organization paid off in the end. The couple finished their vows long before their wedding day, so the process didn't add any extra stress to the wedding plans. Outstanding work, Sam and Pam.

Putting pen to paper can be the hardest part, especially if you don't write regularly. Basic creative writing techniques, like making lists and creating outlines, can help inexperienced writers and professionals alike to gather their thoughts, get organized, and get started. By embracing these techniques, you'll be guided through the process and, hopefully, prevent any unnecessary additional stress.

It's time to put your pen to paper and embrace the lessons that Sam and Pam's process has to teach you.

Find a starting point.

Getting started is hard. Your vows have lived in your head up until this point, and now that it's time to write, you'd rather sip a cocktail and keep dreaming. Sam and Pam eased their way into vow writing by making lists, and it gave them great content to work with. So that's where you'll start.

Begin by making a list of the qualities that you love about your partner. They can be obvious or subtle, broad or specific, or everything in between. Take your time on this exercise as it might take a few days for you to create a complete list. After you're done, write a short example for each of the qualities you listed. See the example below:

Quality: He's kindhearted.

Example: He treats everyone he encounters with kindness and respect. He holds the door open for strangers, asks cashiers about their day, and treats people with patience and understanding, even when he gets cut off in rush hour traffic.

The next thing you'll want to do is highlight a few of your favorite qualities. After you've done that, you'll use them to get started on your actual vows. Here is a vow based on the example above:

Vow: You are compassionate and so full of love. Everyone who comes in contact with you is better for it. You are the most kindhearted person I've ever met, and I promise to reciprocate and learn from that kindness as best as I can.

Repeat this process for every quality you highlighted on your list. By the end of this exercise, you'll have some great content. Keep in mind that you'll end up with more content than you can use in your vows, so you'll need to pick and choose your favorite qualities, examples, and lines.

Next, it's time to think about the interdependent nature of your relationship. Now that you have a partner, your life isn't the same. You're no longer ordering in for one…with no excuse to order two desserts for yourself to meet the $25 delivery minimum. Your life only revolved around your needs and desires at first, but now, someone else is in the mix. This next list should reflect these changes.

How do you and your partner support each other? Think about the ways you're supportive throughout the day, and then think big picture. How do you make each other better? What does your partner do to support your dreams? In what ways do you encourage each other to be the best versions of yourselves?

This second list will help you identify how your relationship functions practically and how you and your partner support each other. While you won't use all of this information in your vows, this exercise will provide you with a ton of great content to choose from.

It feels good to put pen to paper, doesn't it? You can find more writing exercises related to this section in your Wedding Vow Journal.

Dive a little deeper.

You chose to marry your partner for countless reasons, some of which you probably don't consciously realize. Sam and Pam wanted to dive deeper and explore the things below the surface, so they spent time considering the more complex and nuanced parts of their relationship. That's what this section is all about.

It's time for you to dive a little deeper.

How do you and your partner support each other emotionally? A healthy emotional connection is essential to having a healthy relationship. What have you learned about yourself now that you have someone supporting you in these ways? You can learn a lot by looking at your emotional state before and after you met your partner. What's changed? Asking yourself questions like this will help you write meaningful vows.

The last thing you'll want to think about is your spiritual connection to your partner. How do you feel spiritually tied to this person you're about to give your life to? Do you think your partner is your soul mate? Explore this idea, and write down your thoughts. The term "soul mate" gets a bad rap, but according to a poll done by the Rutgers University's National Marriage Project, about 88% of single Americans in their 20s believe there is a "special person" out there for them.[10]

Create an outline.

If there was a vow-writing secret sauce, this would be it.

Any English professor will tell you to start with an outline, so this is really a stolen idea. If you're a big fan of efficiency (and who isn't?), then you'll appreciate this part of the process since it will make the hard part much easier. After Pam and Sam created an outline, they were able to organize their thoughts and finish their vows with plenty of time to spare.

Outlines add flow to your structure and structure to your tone and give you guidance when you sit down to write your vows. Keep in mind that no two outlines are alike. You'll want to write in a way that's easy for you to understand and work from, and that varies from person to person.

Sam and Pam's outline was simple, but it worked for them. Still not sure what to do? Check out the example on the right.

Outline Example

- Why I Picked You
  - You're beautifully selfless
  - You're strong willed & fight for what you want
  - I think it's cute when you're stubborn
  - I've never met another person who I connect with like I do with you
- Insert Story About My Grandparents Inspiring Love Story
- Why I Think This Is Going To Work
  - We both value our faith & families
  - We're both open to learning and growing through challenges in our relationship
  - We share the belief that selflessness is a critical foundation for marriage
  - We're willing to put in the work that it takes
- The Promises I Want To Make
  - I promise to love you more than anyone in the world
  - I promise to never go to bed angry
  - I promise to try to be understanding even when I think you're being a crazy person
  - I promise to seek wholeness as an individual so that I'm not relying on you to complete me
- Include Lines From Traditional Methodist Wedding Vows

Dig in

Jay & May

Friends called them polar opposites, but Jay and May preferred the term "perfect counterparts."

Their jobs, hobbies, and even their tastes in movies were on opposite ends of the spectrum. Jay was a socially anxious software developer. May was an office manager at an elementary school who loved people, especially children (whom she called tiny humans). Fate had some work to do with these two. Due to their drastically different lives, the likelihood of them meeting was slim.

Flu season brought Jay and May to the pharmacy on a Friday night, an incident they believed was too amazing to be a coincidence. They made small talk about their sickness, he asked her about the medicine in her hand, she overshared about her nasal passages, and the two exchanged numbers.

On their first date, they went out for pizza—pizza makes all awkwardness less painful. One date turned into two, which quickly turned into five, and the romance grew from there. It was kindled by shared goals and values. Jay and May both came from good families with similar religious beliefs, and they wanted to have a family of their own. They also wanted to retire early enough to travel the world without having to deal with overactive bladders, achy joints, or 7 pm bedtimes.

The differences in their personalities occasionally led to conflict, but they learned how to communicate through it. They had a deep respect for each other, and when their differences failed them, communication wouldn't. Jay and May worked to make their relationship work, and they were better individuals for it.

By the time they got engaged, they had been dating for over two and a half years. Jay proposed in the spot where they'd met, surrounded by flu meds and pharmacy workers. He told her that he'd known she was the one during her rant about nasal spray and that their unconventional story was evidence they were meant to be. It wasn't a classic fairytale proposal, but May wouldn't have had it any other way.

The couple knew they would have a long engagement, so they put off a lot of the wedding plans until the last minute. May wasn't really a planner, and Jay wanted to be involved as little as possible. They didn't even talk about wedding vows until they were planning their ceremony three weeks out.

May and Jay's parents had used the traditional Catholic vows in their ceremonies, so the couple agreed to combine traditional and original vows. And since Jay was a terrible writer in school, the couple agreed to work together.

The first night they sat down to work on their vows, Jay and May were bouncing ideas off of each other in a brainstorming session that would impress even Don Draper.[11] May would say something, Jay would add to it, and then they'd celebrate the brilliance they were creating. After about fifteen minutes, though, they were losing steam, and they didn't have a sassy, 1960s-style secretary to hold their calls or bring them coffee.

Their productivity plummeted. In their discouragement, they decided to call it a night and go out for pizza—pizza heals all wounds. They agreed to give it another try the next day.

During their next writing session, the couple came up with a plan. They would discuss all of the details of their relationship—their past, present, and future—and then, they would write down the highlights of what they discussed. This technique would help them cover all of their bases, and it would give them plenty of material to work with.

Jay and May started from the beginning. They had a blast talking about the night they met, their first date, their first kiss, and the first time they said, "I love you." Jay knew he wanted to include something about the pharmacy in his vows, and May wanted to mention when she'd known she loved him, which was after she broke her finger and he came over every day to wash her dishes.

After they talked about the past, they spent time on the present and analyzed their relationship in its current state.

They'd improved so much as a couple over the years, and they were proud of how far they had come. They were better at communicating through conflict, supporting each other in their weaknesses, and encouraging one another to grow as individuals. Their love was stronger than ever.

The last thing the couple discussed was the future. Their previous discussions gave them a better idea of the promises they wanted to make to each other, and they enjoyed dreaming about what was to come. They spent time picturing their marriage five, ten, and even fifty years in the future, and all four of their imaginary children were beautiful, well-rounded individuals who hung out at the pharmacy to meet their future spouses.

Their plan was a success. Their discussions gave them plenty of material to work with, so they didn't have to deal with another discouraging brainstorming session. When they finished their vows, they went out for pizza—pizza makes all victories sweeter. Incredible work, Jay and May.

Even when your love is strong and your story is romantic, it can be difficult to come up with things to write in your wedding vows. Trains of thought get derailed, ideas turn sour, and enlightening brainstorming sessions come to an end. That's when your only option is to dig into the details of your relationship, and using a timeline approach is one of the easiest ways to do it.

Start digging in with these lessons from Jay and May.

Talk about the past.

Every love story began somewhere, and while your wedding day places emphasis on where you're headed, it's just as important to remember where you came from. Jay and May's story began in a pharmacy during flu season. Yours might have started with an exchange of smiles, an unplanned interaction, or even a setup. Whatever it was, these first interactions eventually compelled you and your partner to get married, which is kind of a big deal.

Although your wedding vows aren't the time to dive into the details of various situations, there are a few special pieces of your history that are worth sharing...and a few that aren't. Your guests would love to hear about the moment after your first kiss when you realized you'd found your soul mate. They wouldn't love to hear about the drama with your ex that led you to make your relationship Facebook-official.

You probably see the difference.

Are there any utterly romantic moments from the beginning of your relationship that you want to share? Have you and your partner been through something challenging that changed your relationship for the better? What about situations that made you realize you never want to do life without this person? Since you can't include everything, brainstorm the highlights that are worth mentioning. You have a five-minute max, remember?

If you're still wondering how to incorporate your love story into your wedding vows, check out the guide and examples in your Wedding Vow Journal.

Talk about the present.

Now that you've spent time thinking about your history, it's time to focus on where you're currently at as a couple. Since you met your partner, you've probably grown in countless ways, both together and as individuals. Discuss things like how you deal with hardship, handle conflict, and complement each other. When Jay and May had this discussion, they realized just how far they had come together.

To get started, ask yourself the following questions:

How have you grown together and as individuals?

What habits do you and you partner have in place to maintain healthy communication?

How do you show your love to each other?

How do you handle conflict?

As you explore these details, you'll gain clarity around the current state of your relationship and your identity as a couple. Once you have a clear picture of where you're at, vow-writing gets a lot easier. Highlight your strengths, and address your weaknesses, but most of all, be honest with your partner about the active role you'll play in creating a healthy marriage.

Talk about the future.

You didn't have to get married; you wanted to. And your reasons for this decision are most likely related to the future you pictured for yourself. Maybe you couldn't picture it without your partner, or maybe you didn't want to.

Think about the promises you want to make to your partner and where you want your marriage to be in one, five, and even twenty years. What improvements do you hope to make? What issues do you hope to grow through? How do you plan to achieve your goals as individuals and as a couple?

In addition to the big picture promises, include a vow or two with a more detailed theme. You've probably been together long enough to have a basic idea of the interpersonal issues you're going to face. Address those things head on. If you struggle with stubbornness and saying sorry when you're wrong, promise your spouse that you'll work on your pride and practice apologizing. If you know your partner struggles with depression, promise that you'll always be there to love and support him or her, even on the darkest days.

Whether you like it or not, by deciding to marry this person, you started to shape your future. Or, as Bob Dylan more poetically put it, "The future for me is already a thing of the past; you were my first love, and you will be my last."[12]

Find your voice

Lou & Sue

Lou and Sue grew up together in Kalamazoo.... Actually, it was Phoenix, but it really should've been Kalamazoo.

They were "just friends" until the summer after their freshman year in college when Lou showed up on Sue's doorstep with her favorite ice cream in hand. He wanted to take a walk because he had big plans, and those plans involved trying to hold her hand. If she let him, the feelings were mutual. If she didn't, he could play it off. Lou's plan was foolproof, or at least he thought it was.

They held hands several times that summer, but that was the only thing that changed. He wasn't sure if "friends who hold hands" was a real thing, so, to be sure, he took it a step further and kissed her one night on his front porch. She kissed back, and kissing was added to their repertoire of things they did together. Unfortunately, "friends with benefits" is definitely a real thing, so Lou had to be clear about his intentions. A week later, he told Sue he liked her. She replied with "ditto," a word that hadn't been cool in decades, but he was too excited about it to question its cultural relevance.

Their lifelong friendship transitioned easily into a relationship with a foundation of trust already in place. Within a few years, they realized they never wanted to live without each other.

Lou proposed on the porch swing where they'd shared their first kiss.

During the first weeks of their engagement, Lou and Sue decided to write their own wedding vows. Lou didn't love the idea, but he accepted it as a challenge—a challenge that he would tackle as soon as possible, just in case it didn't work out. After he completed his first draft, he read his vows out loud to see how they sounded:

> I love you with a love that shall not grow old. Time will pass, and seasons will change, but they will not alter my love for thee. For I never saw true beauty until you…

He stopped reading. *I thought writing like Shakespeare would make me sound romantic, not sixty-five years old*, Lou thought to himself. Lou removed all of the "shalls" and "thees" and elaborate metaphors. His goal for his next draft was to simplify his writing style. It was easier to write this way, and after he finished, he started to read it out loud:

> I've never met a girl like you, and there's never been a love like ours. When I hug you, I'm holding my whole world in my arms. My mom told me to follow my dreams, and I plan to follow you around for the rest of my life.

"What's happening?" Lou whispered under his breath. He thought he was doing better to simplify his language, but once he started reading his vows out loud, he realized he sounded like an adolescent who was crushing on the girl sitting behind him in math class. Lou was annoyed with his lack of progress, so he just started writing whatever popped into his head.

You're my best friend…too obvious.

You're beautiful, inside and out…too cliché.

You are my sunshine...too juvenile.

I can be your hero...too Enrique Iglesias.

Lou was at his breaking point. He called his fiancée for advice.

"Be yourself, find your voice, and say what you want to say. Whatever you come up with will be perfect," Sue said gently.

As much as he appreciated her kindness, Sue's response made him want to drop his phone in the toilet...and flush it. Lou wasn't sure how to be himself, especially on paper. So he called Sue again and asked her to help him make a list of his most obvious qualities.

"You're determined. You love to have fun. You love me so well...." Her voice trailed off as she thought about the things that made Lou who he was. Everything she said resonated with him.

"So my vows should be resolute, fun, and romantic?" he asked.

Sue smiled. "That sounds about right."

After their conversation, Lou felt like he was finally getting started. Everything he'd written before was fabricated or borrowed. He hadn't been writing from a place of vulnerability or authenticity, so nothing sounded quite right.

As he read his final draft out loud, he breathed a sigh of relief. There were still adjustments that needed to be made, but he had finally found his voice. Lou had expected that writing his own wedding vows would be a challenge, but he hadn't known he would have such a hard time not sounding like a fourteen-year-old or a Latin pop star.

Lou and Sue finished their vows and read them to each other for the first time on their wedding day. They brought each other to tears and shared a beautiful, meaningful moment. Now that's how it's done, Lou and Sue.

Your vows should feel true to your voice, not someone else's. Lou would have saved a lot of time if he'd known how to "be himself" from the start. The process of finding your voice begins with reflection and ends with reading your vows out loud to make sure that what you wrote sounds like something you would actually say. That sounds easy enough, right?

Don't write vows that feel forced or inauthentic. Find your voice with these lessons from Lou and Sue's story.

Define it.

One of the most common mistakes new writers make is to lose their voice in their work. It's easy to imitate your favorite authors or bloggers whenever you're writing, but when it comes to your wedding vows, it's crucial that you sound like yourself. Lou didn't even know what his voice was supposed to sound like when he got started, and it's okay if that's how you feel too.

There's nothing more awkward than a bride or a groom reading original wedding vows that sound like they were written by Shakespeare.... "My bounty is as boundless as the sea, my love as deep; the more I give to thee, The more I have, for both are infinite."[13] As a matter of fact, the only case in which this would be acceptable would be if you or your partner teach British Literature, and even then, you should probably refrain.

You probably see where this is headed. The goal is to sound like yourself on your wedding day when you're reading your vows, and choosing a writing style and using verbiage that's true to who you are will help with that.

But how do you know what your voice should sound like?

You define it.

First, think about how you would describe yourself. Are you funny, artistic, or outspoken? Reserved, romantic, or eccentric? Write down a short list of your qualities, and ask your partner to review it and make adjustments with you.

Next, ask yourself if the structure and tone that you decided on earlier in the book are true to who you are. If they're spot on, that's great, but if they're a little off, you'll want to rethink them. For example, if you wanted your wedding vows to be a comedic monologue, but you consider yourself reserved, you should probably make some changes.

The last thing you'll want to do is begin brainstorming your usual verbiage. Think of specific words that you say a lot in conversation or use to describe your relationship to an outsider. Then think about how you communicate. Are you a storyteller? Are you sarcastic? Do you communicate directly? Your awareness of these things will help you further define your voice.

Refine what you have.

Now that you've defined your voice, you'll need to refine your vows and make them sound like you. Lou wrote several drafts before he got it right, so don't feel discouraged if it takes you a few tries; unless you're a professional, it probably will.

Begin by adding words that you say frequently and removing words that you don't. Then adjust sentences to sound like something you would say. You'll want to make sure that your personality shows throughout your vows and that the flow feels natural to you.

If you've already written the bulk of your vows, don't stress. It just means you already know what you want to say, and that frees you up to focus on how you say it.

Read it out loud.

The best way to know whether your vows sound like you or not is to read them out loud…preferably not on the train or in a coffee shop. You would hate to cause innocent bystanders to fall in love with you, wouldn't you? That poor barista showed up to work to make coffee, not to get her heart broken.

As simple as it sounds, this is a technique that professional writers use to make sure their personality is present in their copy. This is how Lou knew he was doing it wrong and, eventually, how he knew he had gotten it right.

After you've finished writing and adjusting for voice, read your vows out loud again. This practice will give you a whole new perspective. When you recognize a sentence that needs work, adjust it and reread it until you get it right. Then move on to the next one.

It's all a part of the process, and at the end of it, you'll have original wedding vows that are worthy of your voice.

make adjustments

Jim & Kim

Jim grew up in the Midwest with three brothers and a little sister. His dad was an anchor on ESPN, so his life naturally revolved around sports seasons. For example, it wasn't autumn; it was football season. He learned the importance of strength, competition, and protein supplements at a young age. To say masculinity was a core value in his home would be an understatement.

Jim was a star athlete in high school, and it paid for his college. After he graduated, he took a job in Chicago. That's when he met Kim.

Jim was at a networking event for work when he saw her. Kim was the prettiest girl in his row, so he came up with different reasons to talk to her throughout the event.

"My pen is under your seat."

"Is the Wi Fi working?"

"It's cold in here."

After a full day of attempts, Jim gave himself away when he said, "I lost my phone; can you call it?" Kim knew what he was up to, but she played along. She thought he was cute.

When the event was over, Jim left with Kim's phone number. He knew she was from out of town, so he decided not to call. He wasn't interested in anything complicated or long distance.

Jim spent a lot of his free time at sports bars with his brothers and buddies from college. They'd bet on games, drink craft beer, and get drunk enough to get thrown out at least twice a year. The one time Kim did come up in conversation, Jim told his brother, "She's hot but not long-distance hot."

Four years after they met, Kim was transferred to the company's Chicago branch where Jim worked. He almost choked on a cough drop the first time she walked through the front door. His memory must have failed him before, because she was *definitely* long-distance hot.

When their manager introduced them, Kim acted like she didn't remember Jim. After all, she had been waiting for him to call her for four years, and he never did. She wasn't about to act like that was ok.

She enjoyed ignoring him at first, frequently "forgetting" his name to make a point. He slowly wore on her with his kindness and flirtatious advances. It didn't help that she was lonely in a new city. A few months in, she admitted that she remembered him…and that she had waited for him to call.

When she did, Jim asked her out for coffee. She agreed.

It wasn't long before Jim was missing the game to spend time with her. When he did show up, the guys could tell he was restless to be somewhere else. They asked if it was serious, and at first, Jim didn't know how to respond. But when he started bringing Kim to the sports bar with him, they had their answer.

After two years of dating and missing games, Jim proposed on Christmas day.

The couple wanted to have a summer wedding, which gave them six months to plan. They didn't discuss their wedding vows until one month before their big day, at which point Kim expressed her desire to write original vows. Jim complied without a second thought. He'd been a great writer in school, so he figured he could knock them out quickly and without a hitch. Jim and Kim decided on their vow structure, tone, and other details together, but they wanted to reveal their final drafts on their wedding day.

Every time Jim sat down to write, he was overwhelmed by his feelings for Kim. He wondered how he'd gotten so lucky, and he powerfully articulated his thoughts into words. The first time he read his final vows all the way through, he was moved to tears.

As soon as he realized he was crying, he knew he had written meaningful and vulnerable vows that touched him emotionally... without his consent. It freaked him out. There was no way he could lose control in front of his family like that. He imagined his brothers laughing to themselves while he tearfully read his vows and his father shaking his head in disappointment. Jim knew he couldn't let that happen—so he rewrote his vows.

He cut out the parts that were too vulnerable, and he replaced them with vows he found online. They were just as romantic, but they didn't pull at his heartstrings like the words he'd written himself. He wasn't proud of his decision, but he didn't have a choice.

Jim's sister had promised a week earlier to give him feedback on his vows, and the next day, she came over. After he finished reading them to her, she said nothing.

"What do you think?" Jim asked.

"I think you could do better," she replied. "They're pretty generic."

Growing up with four brothers, Jim's sister had learned to speak her mind. She wasn't one to sugarcoat anything. Jim decided to tell her about his first draft and its effects on him. He then proceeded to tell her why uncontrollable emotions weren't an option.

"Kim should be your priority, not your pride," his sister stated bluntly. "Now read me your first draft."

He read her his original vows. By the end, they were both emotional. Jim knew his sister was right, so he cut out all of the generic, borrowed lines. It meant more to him to say heartfelt vows to Kim on their wedding day than it did to appear tough or unmoved in front of his family.

When the wedding day rolled around, Jim's nerves were all over the place. But when he saw Kim walking towards him down the aisle, he felt calm. Nothing in the world mattered more to him than his bride.

As she read her vows to him, Jim felt tears well up in his eyes, and when he read his, he let them fall. After they finished reading, Jim noticed sniffling behind him. He turned around to see all of his brothers wiping tears from their cheeks. His words had moved his family just as they had moved him.

Jim's shock quickly turned into gratitude. He was thankful for his sister's honest feedback and for his bride who inspired the words…and who was *definitely* long-distance hot.

After the ceremony, Jim and Kim each shared their appreciation for what the other had written. They were proud that they had written original vows that were honest, vulnerable, and powerful enough to move their wedding guests to tears. Good work, Jim and Kim.

It's easy to feel the pressure of wedding vow writing. They're some of the most important words you'll ever say, and you're going to say them in front of a large group of family and friends. You might feel hesitant about what you're writing because your partner isn't the only one listening. It's normal to feel that way, especially if your vows make you feel vulnerable. And while your wedding guests aren't your priority, there are a few adjustments that you might need to make for their sake, highlighting the importance of feedback during the writing process.

Learn which adjustments you need to make with these lessons from Jim and Kim's story.

Consider your audience.

After Jim finished his first draft, he remembered his family would be in the audience listening, so he made adjustments.

Even though he did it for the wrong reasons, he acknowledged an important point: Your partner isn't the only one who will be present when you read your vows. While your partner should definitely be your priority, there are a few things you'll want to consider for the sake of your wedding guests. For example:

If you share something too vulnerable, your guests might feel uncomfortable.

If your vows are too cryptic or full of inside jokes, your guests will be confused.

If your vows get too sexual or intimate, you risk making your guests feel awkward.

If there's a line in your vows that you're not sure about, get feedback. Ask your partner or someone close to you if the questionable line is appropriate or not. If it's not, consider adjusting it to be more crowd-friendly.

One way to decide whether you should include a line or not is to ask yourself, "Would I want this remembered ten years from now?" It's not likely anyone is going to remember your vows in ten years…unless you say something awkward or inappropriate. Then they might. Try not to give your guests (and your partner) something unfortunate to think about when they remember your wedding day.

Remove the excess.

After you finish your first draft, odds are you have way more content than you need. Your goal is to keep your vows between one and five minutes, but really, you should aim for them to be between two and three. Time yourself as you read them out loud to determine how much you'll need to remove.

There's nothing worse than writing a powerful set of vows and then surrounding them with fluff that causes them to be ineffective and drag on and on. It's easy to ramble, especially when you're nervous, but it can be detrimental to your overall message.

The best way to prevent yourself from writing vows that drag on too long is to stay within the time limit. If you've gone over, then you know you need to remove some parts.

Deciding what to remove isn't easy, especially if you feel attached to what you have. Start by removing unnecessary words and details. Then grab a highlighter, and decide which lines you absolutely cannot do without. This will leave you with the dispensable parts, and you can decide from there what to cut and what to keep.

After Jim decided to remove the generic, borrowed lines from his vows, he was left with non-boring, tear inducing wedding-vow gold.

Get feedback.

One of the best ways to know if your vows are cry-worthy or cringe-worthy is to get a second opinion from someone on the outside of your writing process.

Jim's choice to get feedback from his sister had a huge effect on his end result.

It's hard to judge your own work, especially if you're one of those people who's inclined to think your work is awesome. You won't know if words came off in the way you intended them to or if they flowed well together. If you're not a professional, you might even consider having someone edit your work. The last thing you want to do is read vows on your wedding day that are all over the map or feel incomplete.

Language is an imperfect tool we use to send and receive messages, and the written word is forever. Don't assume your vows flow well and communicate your thoughts perfectly just because you wrote from the heart. Give yourself the opportunity for feedback just in case things did get a little weird.

So who should you ask for feedback?

If you and your partner decided to team up on the vow-writing process, or if you're using a structure that requires more collaboration, then you can ask each other. But if you decided to reveal your vows to your partner on your wedding day, then you'll need to ask someone you respect who knows you well, like a close friend or family member.

Once you've chosen someone to give you feedback, have a list of questions prepared. Here are some examples of what you might ask:

1. Do my vows sound like I wrote them?

2. Were they too intimate or not personal enough?

3. What areas could be improved?

4. Did my vows flow together well?

5. Am I missing anything?

When you're asking for feedback, keep an open mind, and do your best not to get defensive. At the end of the day, you can say whatever you want, but it's wise to hear out the person who agreed to help you. Your vows are too important to fly solo.

Finishing touches

Bill & Jill

Bill and Jill planned their entire wedding in five months. There were no boxes left unchecked, no undone tasks in the wedding binder. If preparation could be perfect, they would have been perfectly prepared.

They were model Type-A personalities, a commonality that can be both *really* good and *really* bad. Bill grew up in a military home where he learned to prepare for all possible circumstances, and Jill had two younger sisters who had taught her to be patient, protective, and very much in control. Sure, they butted heads more often because of it, but they were fiercely dedicated and loved each other deeply.

The couple decided to write their own vows, despite their mutual distaste for public speaking, because they wanted to personalize their wedding ceremony. They spent countless hours writing and editing. When they were finished, they read their vows out loud over and over again until they were no longer stumbling over words or reading too fast. To ease the pain of public speaking, they took an hour-long e-course to learn some techniques for powerful vow delivery. Again, perfectly prepared.

Unfortunately, preparation can only do so much good, and no amount of it could have helped Bill and Jill on their wedding day.

Jill's morning wasn't off to a great start. Her little sisters' bickering was irritating her more than it usually did. She was patient, yes, but on the morning of her wedding, she was done hearing it after the first two hours.

"If you two don't stop fighting, I'm uninviting you to my wedding," Jill said. She was kind of serious, and her sisters could sense it.

At that same time, Bill was hugging his third groomsman goodbye outside. A family emergency had come up the night before, so the groomsman had to catch a flight out the morning of the wedding. Bill was understanding of the situation, but now he had to fill in the gaps at the ceremony and reception.

The couple had planned to take their wedding photos three hours prior to the ceremony. At that time, the bride and groom shared a sweet "first look" moment that was caught on camera. On their way back to their wedding party, they discussed their options for the missing groomsman. They didn't love making last-minute changes, but they didn't have a choice.

As they were walking and talking, Jill's veil got caught on a bush and yanked her backwards. She managed to stay on her feet, but there was a rip in her veil where it had caught. Jill would have cried, but she'd paid too much for her makeup to mess it up before the ceremony.

Forty-five minutes before the wedding, the officiant had yet to arrive. He had technically passed "late" thirty minutes ago, so by this point, Bill was about to lose it. On his third try, the officiant answered his phone only to report a blown tire without a spare. He had to wait on his ride, but he'd arrive shortly.

"Well, I can't hit a clergyman," Bill said to his best man after he got off the phone, frustrated by the delay.

The groomsmen were about to be cued to enter the ceremony, so Bill's best man revealed mini-bottles of Jack Daniel's that he had stolen from the bar earlier that day to calm Bill's nerves and, now, to ease his frustration. They toasted to Bill's final moment of freedom and the woman that would become his wife. Bill was overwhelmed with gratitude for his fiancée, his friends, and miniature bottles of stolen liquor.

They heard the music playing, but the wedding planner hadn't signaled the groomsmen to begin the processional. Bill had a feeling something wasn't right, and sure enough, the wedding planner was busy attending to an unhappy grandmother who didn't appreciate her second row seat when the music started playing. The playlist was perfectly timed for the processional, so it had to be started over in order to work.

At this point, Bill was all out of calm, but that changed the moment he saw his bride. In that moment, he realized just how unimportant all that other stuff was. Jill was the most beautiful thing he'd ever seen.

The officiant opened the ceremony with a prayer—and an unsilenced cell phone rang. Bill and Jill looked up at each other, unsure of how to respond, and the couple burst into laughter. Seeing the pair unable to control themselves, the officiant paused the prayer. Bill had briefed him on the day's happenings before the ceremony, so he used this opportunity to commend the couple for enduring a day full of "unexpected interruptions."

When the time came for the wedding vows, Bill and Jill confidently read them aloud.

"Jill, I love every part of you, even the parts I can't figure out. I promise to cherish you and the person you're going to become…."

"Bill, I am your biggest fan. I promise to respect you even when I don't feel like it and to love you even when it hurts…."

During the five minutes in which the couple read their vows, there wasn't a dry eye in the room. Their words were genuine and powerful. A day full of chaos had come to a halt, and the only thing that mattered was the commitment Bill and Jill had showed up to make.

Things didn't go as planned after the ceremony either. Jill got a wine stain on her dress, one of Bill's groomsmen had too much to drink, and other unfavorable things occurred, but the couple didn't notice. They were too wrapped up in each other and their big day. After the reception, Jill's mother approached their getaway car with a gift before they left.

"I really hope this isn't a wedding night gift, Mom…," Jill said as she warily received the gift from her mother.

"It isn't," her mom replied, "But if you need me to run to the pharmacy to get you some…"

"No!" Jill interrupted her before she could finish, unsure and mildly disturbed by what her mother was about to say.

Jill opened the gift and found their wedding vows beautifully framed. The gift was incredibly meaningful because the entire mood of their wedding day shifted drastically after they exchanged vows. They were no longer bothered by the chaos and frustrating circumstances. Instead, they were able to refocus on what really mattered.

"Things didn't go perfectly today," Jill's mother said, "but weddings can't be perfect, and marriage can't be either. Your vows saved your wedding day, and they'll save your marriage over and over again."

Bill and Jill were speechless. She was right. No amount of preparation could have prevented the problems they'd encountered that day, and nothing could guarantee a perfect, problem-free marriage either. As they drove away, they laughed and dreamed about the future. They couldn't wait to begin their less-than-perfect, problem-filled life together. Best of luck, Bill and Jill.

This young couple learned a valuable lesson. You have to roll with the punches and be committed to endure the trials that will inevitably come your way in your marriage. That's why wedding vows are so important in the first place. When things go wrong and it's easier to give up than it is to move forward, your vows are the glue that holds your marriage together.

In addition to the lesson Bill and Jill learned on their wedding day, there are a few practical things that can be learned from their story. Get ready to wrap it up and add some finishing touches.

Practice, practice, practice.

When your vows are complete, it's time to focus on your delivery. Bill and Jill spent a ton of time practicing their vows before their big day. If you're not in the habit of talking to yourself, this part might feel weird, but the best way to practice delivering your original, tear-inducing, non-boring wedding vows is to read them out loud.

Over. And over. And over again.

As you read your vows out loud, you become more familiar with them, and as you become more familiar, you start to see where to add emphasis. Inflections, pauses, and phrasing are all ways to add emphasis to certain words or lines in your vows. If you've never taken an acting class, you might need a quick vocabulary lesson.

Emphasis: force or intensity of expression that gives... importance to something[14]

Inflection: a rise or fall in the sound of a person's voice...a change in the pitch or tone[15]

Pause: a temporary stop[16]

(If you didn't know this word, you probably shouldn't be writing your vows...or maybe you've never owned a VCR or DVD player. If that's the case, you may proceed.)

Phrasing: the particular words or the order of words that are used to express something[17]

As you read your vows out loud, ask yourself where you want to place emphasis and how. Do you want to add a pause after you say a certain word? Will your voice fall or rise as you read a certain sentence? Have you arranged your words in a particular order to emphasize them?

A lot of these things should come naturally as you read your vows out loud. Be sure not to add emphasis in a place where it feels unnatural for you. If you're still not sure what or how to emphasize, get feedback from someone who knows you well.

Prepare yourself for the delivery.

You're almost to the finish line. Well, at least this one. Your wedding day might still be six months away. If so, bravo! Although it's more likely that it's coming up...like next week. Either way, it's time to get prepared for your vow delivery.

First, you need to decide if you'll be reading or memorizing your vows. Unless you're an actor or professional speaker, it's wise to go the reading route. When you memorize your vows, you risk forgetting something important, and you add extra pressure to a day that's already filled with nerves and expectations. If you do decide to memorize them, begin as early as possible, and consider using a notecard with an outline just in case nerves get the best of you.

Bill and Jill tried to be "perfectly prepared" for their wedding day, so they went the extra mile with a public speaking e-course. You probably don't need to go that far, but here's what you do need to keep in mind while you're delivering your vows.

You are going to be nervous.

It happens to everyone. Some people get sick to their stomach, and others get shaky hands. You know how your body responds to nerves, so you should be mentally prepared for it. Practice your vows out loud to minimize shaky vocals, chug Pepto-Bismol for your stomach, and take a deep breath or two before you begin. Whatever you need to do, do it. You'll be thankful you were proactive about it.

Make eye contact...with the right person.

Your officiant, your wedding party, and even a few of your wedding guests might be in your line of vision while you're delivering your vows. Try not to look at them. Your eyes should move back and forth between your vows and your partner. Wandering eyes imply that you're distracted or not listening, even if you're just nervous. Distracted brides and grooms *don't* make the best wedding photos.

Don't be afraid to cry.

If you can't stand the thought of shedding a tear in front of the brother that relentlessly made fun of you for being a crybaby for the last twenty years, you're not alone. Crying is a vulnerable thing, and the words you wrote in your wedding vows are vulnerable too. As a matter of fact, if vulnerability isn't really your thing, you may want to reconsider having any wedding guests at all—or you can accept the fact that your ceremony is going to require you to be vulnerable...which is probably your better option.

Most couples shed a tear or two on their wedding day, so if you feel them coming on at any point, don't fight it. Let 'em fall. Crying couples *do* make the best wedding photos.

Make a clean copy.

In this case, a clean copy is a finalized version of your wedding vows. There won't be any markups or additions, and the font will be large and legible. Your clean copy should be printed or written where you plan to read them on your big day. Consider using a small journal or notebook so that your pages don't get mixed up in the chaos of the ceremony or fly away in the wind.

The wind will always win a war with loose sheets of paper. Always.

Keep in mind that your clean copy will likely make its way into your wedding photography. You'll want to choose a pretty journal or notebook that goes with the feel of your wedding décor. Plus, if you decide to keep your vows after the ceremony, they'll be stored in a nice-looking notebook. Bill and Jill's handwritten vows were in such great condition that Jill's mother was able to frame them, a gift they treasured long after their wedding day.

Conclusion

Ah…wedding vows, the most romantic part of the ceremony.

That's all they were at the start of this book: a romantic idea. Now that you've pulled back the curtain, you see the thought, work, and detail that go into the process of writing original, tear-inducing, non-boring wedding vows. And it wasn't so bad, right?

Unless it's been forced upon you…then you're probably reading this conclusion and seething that there was nothing in the book about how wrong it is to force your fiancé to write wedding vows despite his or her objection. If that's the case, do not, under any circumstances, force or manipulate your partner into writing original wedding vows. That would be cruel and inhumane.

There. Now highlight that part, and show it to your partner. You're welcome…. You can show your appreciation with a rave review.

If you weren't forced to read this book, then you probably noticed the hardest part of the whole process isn't the process at all but the timing of it. While you're writing your vows, you're usually in the trenches of wedding planning. You're being bombarded with hundreds of thoughts and questions about your big day, and you're being asked to make commitments and decisions regularly that have nothing to do with your vows.

Should you do dinner or hors d'oeuvres? How long should your first kiss be, and should you add a little tongue? Will anyone get shamelessly drunk at your reception and ruin everything? Is that seriously how you spell "hors d'oeuvres?" It's hard to focus on vow writing when you have so many things vying for your attention.

But you did it. You finished the book, and even though there's no such thing as a "professional wedding vow writer," you're one step closer to it. The lessons you learned from these adorably named couples were meant for novice and professional writers alike. Ideally, you have several weeks or months before your wedding to apply them.

Hopefully, you found all of the information, guidance, and encouragement that you needed to write the most original, tear-inducing, non-boring wedding vows of all time. If you need more hands-on practice and guidance, purchase the companion journal for this edition, *Wedding Vow Journal: Your guide to the most original, tear-inducing, non-boring wedding vows of all time.*

You were brave to pick up this book. Writing original wedding vows can be intimidating and even scary, so your choice to write them anyways is pretty darn commendable.

Congratulations on your big day and on finding someone who inspires you to be brave, work hard, and cry in public. Even if your vows sound unoriginal, bring no one to tears, and bore your wedding guests...you still won.

Acknowledgements

Bobby, thank you for making this project possible. You've heard and supported every dream, and you continue to stand beside me as they come true. Thank you to my supportive parents and in-laws, my inspiring brothers, my Dannenbergs, and my encouraging friends. Y'all are the reason I have the courage to journey through uncharted territory.

Huge thanks to my editor, Hilary Gunning, for your thorough, insightful work and your encouragement. To my designer, Emily Wells, for understanding my vision and producing breathtaking work time after time. To my friend, Claire Linic, who agreed to read and review my manuscript before she knew what she was getting herself into. To my mentor, Jennifer Martin, who helped me navigate the messy work of personal growth, believing in myself and making my dreams a reality. And, of course, to my designated doodler and overall supporter, Dustin Lindsey.

And to Zach, I couldn't have done this without you consistently and kindly responding to my "I can't" with "Yes, you can."

Appendix

[1] Brown, B. (2012). Daring greatly: How the courage to be vulnerable transforms the way we live, love, parent, and lead. New York, NY: Gotham Books.

[2] Lytton, E. G. (1839). Richelieu, or the Conspiracy: A Play in Five Acts. Paris, France.

[3] Ludwig Erhard. (n.d.). BrainyQuote.com. Retrieved August 23, 2016, from http://brainyquote.com/quotes/quotes/l/ludwigerha194195.html

[4] Grease [Motion picture]. (1978). Hollywood, CA: Paramount Pictures.

[5] Kleon, A. (2012). Steal like an artist: 10 things nobody told you about being creative. New York: Workman Pub.

[6] Gilbert, E. (2006). Eat, pray, love: One woman's search for everything across Italy, India and Indonesia. New York: Viking.

[7] Swift, T. S., & Martin, M. (2012). I Knew You Were Trouble [CD]. Big Machine Records: Scott Borchetta.

[8] Timberlake, J., & Hugo, C. (2003). [Recorded by P. Williams]. Señorita [MP3]. Jive Records: The Neptunes.

[9] Clements, R., & Musker, J. (Directors), & Musker, J., & Ashman, H. (Producers). (1989). The Little Mermaid [Motion picture on VHS]. United States: Buena Vista Pictures Distribution, Inc.

[10] Kelleher, M. (n.d.). Study: Americans Seek Soul-Mate Spouse. Retrieved August 18, 2016, from http://abcnews.go.com/US/story?id=93078

[11] Weiner, M. (Producer). (2007, July 19). Mad Men [Television series]. Los Angeles, California: AMC.

[12] Dylan, B., Campbell, L., Sexton, C., Garnier, T., Kemper, D., & Meyers, A. (2001). Bye and Bye. On *Love and Theft* [CD]. New York City, New York: Columbia Records.

[13] Shakespeare, W., & Evans, H. A. (1886). Romeo and Juliet. London, England: C. Praetorius.

[14] emphasis. 2011. In *Merriam-Webster.com*.

Retrieved May 8, 2011, from http://www.merriam-webster.com/dictionary/emphasis

[15] inflection. 2011. In *Merriam-Webster.com*.

Retrieved May 8, 2011, from http://www.mer

riam-webster.com/dictionary/inflection

[16] pause. 2011. In *Merriam-Webster.com*.

Retrieved May 8, 2011, from http://www.merriam-webster.com/dictionary/pause

[17] phrasing. 2011. In *Merriam-Webster.com*.

Retrieved May 8, 2011, from http://www.merriam-webster.com/dictionary/phrasing

Wedshock

There's more to marriage than happily ever after.

Let's just be honest. One day you're a wild and free bachelor/bachelorette, and the next you're committing to a lifelong roommate…that you share your dreams, money, emotions, and even your toothpaste with. That's nothing short of a gigantic adjustment, and yet, the resources available to help you navigate your newlywed life are microscopic compared to the businesses, publications and experts available to help you plan a wedding, buy a dress, or organize a rehearsal dinner.

Not cool.

That's why we created Wedshock: to support newlyweds in a fun, honest and helpful way while they're experiencing the highs and lows of new marriage. No need to navigate this unpredictable season alone. We've got you.

For Bride-to-be and Newlywed Resources, visit wedshock.com.

Facebook.com/wedshock
Instagram @wedshock
Twitter @wedshock